two hundred:
a sequel

matthew howard

puma concolor aeternus
2016

Two Hundred: A Sequel.

ISBN-10: 1539469743
ISBN-13: 978-1539469742

Our Story So Far

Leonard Elementary
1978-79
KENNETH VINCENT - PRINCIPAL
DIANA COSSIN - ASSISTANT PRINCIPAL
LOU KEMP - KINDERGARTEN

LEAVE SOMETHING FOR THE
IMAGINATION. 2016

CONTENTS

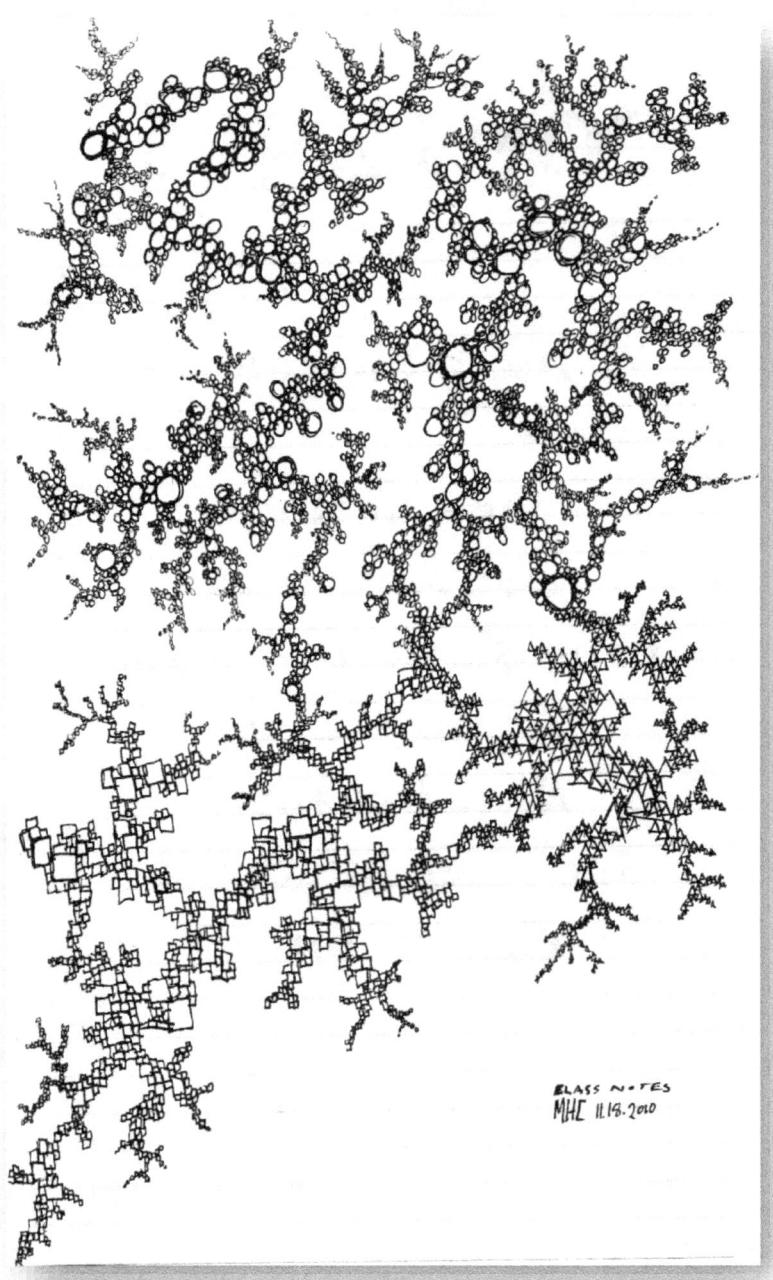

CLASS NOTES
MHE 11.18.2010

INTRODUCTION

Two Hundred is a collection of otherwise unpublished artifacts from my travels, adventures, and explorations during my twenties and thirties—a period which lasted from 1993 to 2013. This is a scrapbook full of fragments and a young man's memories that don't really fit into my other books but for which I still have a great deal of nostalgia.

I can look at any one of these sketches, song lyrics, or brief memoirs and recall when and where I created it, and what was happening in my personal, emotional, and artistic life at that moment. I remember who was with me, sharing experiences and influencing my development as a visual, verbal, and musical artist.

Not all of those recollections make for exciting stories in and of themselves, so I have let their remains stand on their own in these pages. In that regard, it is a decidedly introspective retrospective. On the other hand, the inspirations these artifacts represent continue to inform in no small way my continuing journeys into poetry and fiction.

Every now and then, I like to take a moment to remember where I've been, so I can go somewhere I've never been before. If you'd like to take an intimate look with me into my personal archives, just turn the page.

ONE HAIKU

HAIKU

Give me the damn mic
to growl my manifesto
incoherently.

TWO

ANIMALS

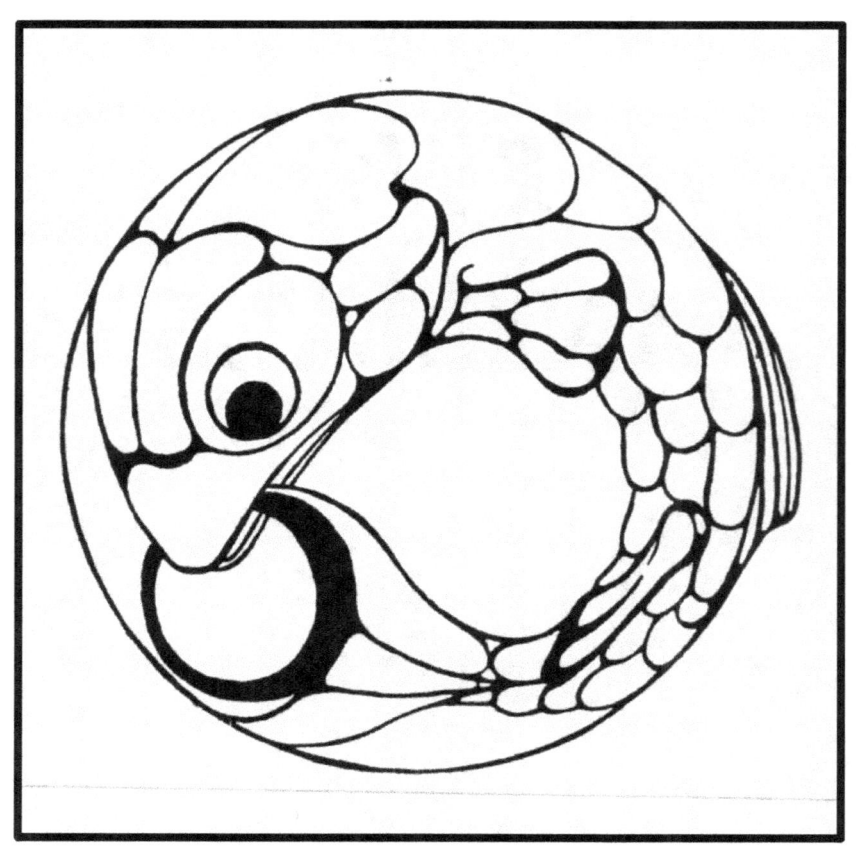

Bird

You last heard the bird as she slept beside you. The song called to you where your bodies lay entwined.

"Where are you going?" she asked. Your movements traced shadows in the diaries of her dreams.

"The bird," you told her. "I need to hear it." You got on your knees and put your head out the open window, listening to catch the melody under the full autumn moon and the crickets taking choruses in the overgrown yard.

✳

Fish

The salmon arrives in the kitchen already gutted, one smooth slit down its belly. To prepare it, you first remove the head by making a small cut with the knife just behind the tiny fins near the head and use a little force to get it through the top of the spine. With the head removed, you slide the knife into the flesh right above the freshly exposed backbone and angle it downward.

As you draw it from right to left, the blade crackles along the spine. With the fish cut in half, you take a hold of it with your hand wrapped in a towel (this cut can be slightly dangerous) and slip the knife up under the backbone, angling the knife upwards this time and making that crackling noise again until the backbone is removed.

The removal of the skin is your favorite part: the smoothness of pulling the fish towards you by the tail as the knife remains still, the blade pointing away from you and the meat just sliding right off the skin. Small sticky scales, so recently alive, remain on your hands even after you wash, sometimes for days, strangely familiar, like a second skin.

THREE BLACKOUT POEMS

silver.

Suddenly

She disappears into

the fire.
and we breathe
the funerals
of   gods.

treasures
such as
the dark red sap of
blood

living in

isolation.

as their

history

the outside world.

has changed.

SEVEN STATES

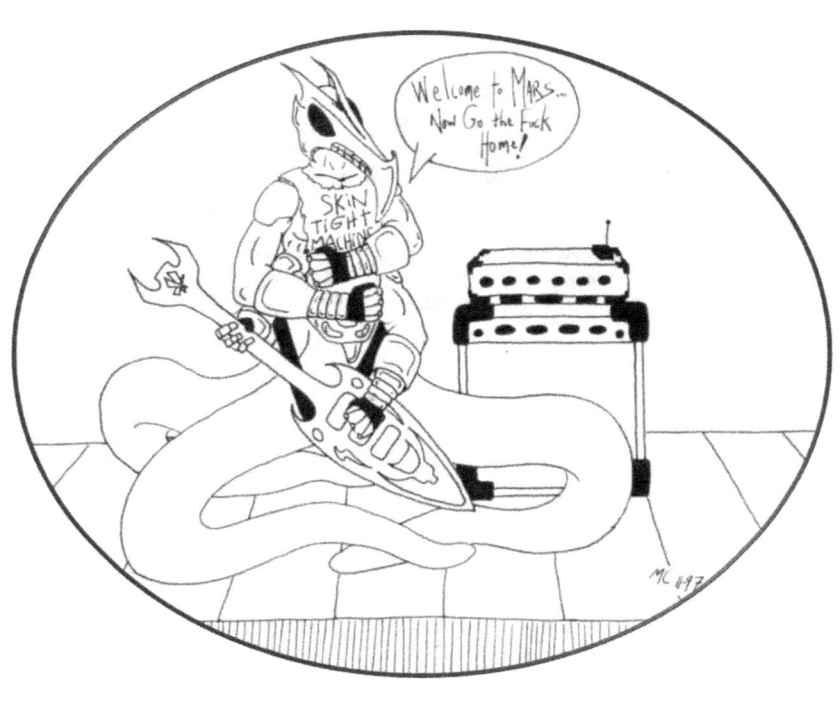

Utah

In the morning, you wake up on Mars. Every other morning of your life, you woke up on Earth like everybody else. Not this morning.

The last thing you remember, the sky bristled with stars until you couldn't stand it anymore, and you passed out in the driver's seat with your hat over your eyes. All the hours of driving blurred together until you didn't know how far you'd gone, only that you'd kept going.

The sunrise bloodies 180 degrees of the horizon before you, a senseless incomprehensible glow. The rearview mirror exposes a wasteland, white, blockaded at the vanishing point by pale blue figures, still and silent. It was easier to get out of the truck ten years ago after a seventeen-hour night of driving. Your black leather boots crush the Martian soil, but it's white, not red. Where are you?

The other side of the sign by the road says, "Bonneville Salt Flats". *Oh!* This shit on the ground is all *salt*. Miles and miles of salt.

You try to wake your passenger, but she's out cold. Too bad for her. Too bad to pass out on Mars and miss it all.

You never see things quite the same way after that. By the age of 50, a man wakes up more than 18,000 times. Most of them, he never remembers.

✳

Nebraska

Exploded tires punctuate the endless Nebraska highway. August afternoon peaks under blatantly naked skies. This truck has no air conditioning but the open windows, no shade from the sun but a bottle of lotion.

19

She drives. You massage the sunscreen into your skin and hair and sweat. 75 miles per hour, kicked back and relaxed. What a luxury. When was the last time you took someone along? Ten years ago? An entire decade? More than 48,000 miles of road comprise the Dwight D. Eisenhower National System of Interstate and Defense Highways. You drove most of them alone.

You moisten her face with a wet cloth. Cool the curve of her cheeks, the back of her neck. Pull her sweater open. Dampen her chest. Wet the glistening slopes of her breasts. Why a black sweater in all this heat? You don't know. You don't ask. You are too busy storing this memory somewhere you can carry it forever: the pink sphere of her cheek, the pleasure in her smile.

Just before sunset, you stop for ice cream. In the shadows of trees, the two of you and the ice cream and your kisses form an oasis in the middle of godforsaken nowhere. Laughter. Laughter like kids, but it's the only ice cream you ever had that was better than when you were a kid, better than most people have in their entire lives.

Was this what you spent ten years looking for? A moment in time to serve as an answer when they ask you why you can't do all the things you are supposed to do? Then here it is: this moment with exactly one long road in, and the future on the other side.

✸

Michigan

In a gesture of welcome, Michigan puts on its most brilliant thundercloud display, and you, you jaded bastard, would have hardly noticed. She's never seen clouds like this on the coast, the rolling, cascading towers in the air. Through her eyes you see it fresh, and you recall in an instant how you once lived life in awe and wonder. How dare you ever forget?

Just for the fun of it, you stay at the sleaziest motel in town until she catches a train back to the coast in three days. The Harmony House, rumored to be many things, immediately earns the nickname Harlotry House. You spend nights reading Kerouac and Cohen and each other by candlelight. Thousands of miles from where you met, you share your words, your lives, your bodies, your secrets, your wishes.

You take her to Lake Pickerel on an overcast day, the only place where you can go skinny dipping at three in the afternoon. It's a weekday, and you have the lake all to yourselves. You entertain her by jumping naked off the dock into the water over and over, giggling like an idiot.

The perfect water. The perfect solitude. The view and its reflections in a perfect mirror. She says, "This is what I will look back on and remember—this lake." And you—you'll try to remember every last bit of it.

✳

California

Her girlfriend always liked to point out that Pythian Castle on H Street used to be a whorehouse. The second-story apartment in Pythian Castle, now empty of whores above the quaint shops and hair salon, boasted a huge bay window. In one direction, you could watch the sun set over the bay and the Samoa Spit. In the other direction, to your left, you could see hills covered in redwood pines and low-lying fog.

It didn't hurt that every babe in town passed by that corner. During rush hour, you would lovingly, drunkenly laugh about how the worst traffic ever got was three cars at a stop sign. After the mechanized, urbanized, freeway hell of San Diego for eighteen months, it was the most beautiful window in the world.

But nothing lasts forever, not even glorious views. When the lease was up, she wanted to move. She stayed with friends for a while. You had a job and figured you'd rough it in your truck for three weeks until the new place opened up. Nights, you cruised up to Trinidad with a bottle of Jack Daniels and a bottle of Coke, getting drunk under the full moon, playing your guitar as loud as you wanted below the stars, with weather just warm enough that when you'd had your fill you could curl up under a blanket in the front seat, pull your leather hat over your eyes, and sleep as long as you wanted.

One afternoon, you were on the beach, lying in the sand, taking in the oncoming sunset. The truck was parked on the cliffs high above. Suddenly, you got an inexplicable chill and decided to leave. On the way to the trail leading back to the truck, you came across a dead snake.

It lay there dead, but nothing had eaten it. It didn't make sense. Birds hadn't touched it. Bugs didn't crawl on it. It lay there stupidly, senselessly, uselessly destroyed. You thought that if you were superstitious, you might read this as an omen of impending doom. Then you thought, *Fuck it—if you go around thinking like that, you'll go nuts.*

At the top of the trail, on the cliffs overlooking the beach, you found your truck's window smashed out completely, lying in "ghetto diamonds" all over the ground. You had little of value in there: blankets, pillows, cassette tapes, an empty bottle, your overnight bag.

The county cops told you that someone had been doing it all night: some punk kids probably, playing a game of smash-and-grab. That's where you go down all the beaches in sequence, smashing windows and grabbing something easily, quickly reached, only to toss it away later. Dumb game.

These particular bastards took only your overnight bag. It might seem like a little thing, like a small and insignificant snake, but everything you had for grooming and hygiene for work, play, and getting laid was in there. The toiletries were never recovered: the scissors, the razors, the soap, the lotion, the condoms, the silicone lubricants. The pointless destruction of it all in a perfectly beautiful place.

✳

California Again

Two weeks later, the two of you drive south to Half Moon Bay to see those fifty-foot waves she heard about. They aren't really that big, but pretty big. You walk down to the edge of the tide in the moonlight and take off your clothes.

She walks into the water as far as she can go without being pulled under. A little farther each time, teasing. She's fine. Crazy, but fine.

You dig a hole in the sand, large enough to sit, deeper than the level of the tide. The water seeps in around her. She sits on her knees, leaning back in the moonlight as you pile wet sand on her naked stomach and her breasts, laughing.

✳

Mississippi

The nice part about your train's catching fire in the middle of the night? You get free breakfast the next morning. At 3 a.m., a gathering of leaves underneath Amtrak #59, the famed "City of New Orleans", bursts into flames. Seven hours out of Chicago, sleepy passengers flee to the lounge car as one watchful fellow calls out, "Wake up, y'all! Somethin' on this muthafucka's on *fire!*"

You find an abandoned box of M&Ms and enjoy a late-night

23

snack with your feet propped up on the little beverage counter below the windows. Lights from the fire trucks race around the ceiling until everyone returns to the coach car.

The next day, all the staff says about the incident is, "Would you like bacon or sausage with your eggs and hash browns, folks?" Free orange juice makes the whole trouble worthwhile.

Your belly is full, and you've got two or three hours to kill before the stop in Jackson. The Mississippi lowlands speed backwards in the windows, enchanting, like a pen pal you fell madly in love with and now meet for the first time. She stretches out beside your train and bats her autumn-brown eyes.

You take your guitar from the overhead luggage rack and play for a while. The hoof beats of the iron horse make for one hell of a rhythm section. You trance out on a crazy little riff in E, running it through the changes in a lazy dream.

Suddenly, a hand rests on your shoulder. It belongs to a voice that says, "You *play* that thing, boy! You get *on* it!" The woman wears a grandmotherly smile. She wants to know if you know the one "that goes like this". She starts singing and you, with a lucky guess on the correct key, pound out three chords for her. "Put somethin' on the bar besides your elbow— Somethin' like a five-dollar bill—Put somethin' on the bar besides your elbow—We can't ring up your elbow on the bill."

The two of you know a few of the same tunes. Together, you run through a bunch of sing-along Baptist choruses.

Then the door of the lounge car opens, and a stream of kids pours in. Today is their lucky day: a field trip on the City of New Orleans. Your singer claps her hands and sings the choruses all over again, what you might call testifyin'.

The car fills with smiling faces and laughter. Some kids know the songs and sing along. Some just clap in time. The performance continues until the next city, where the kids loudly applaud before disembarking to meet their school bus.

As Mississippi races past the train and into your memory, their open-hearted joy in making spontaneous music together lingers in the air. Three chords have rarely been so rewarding to play.

✳

Georgia

Fugazi came from Washington, D.C. and issued records on their own label, DisChord. DisChord started up when Ian's hard-core straight-edge band Minor Threat was making records in the 1980s. One day in the Spring of 1996, after writing a letter to the band, I got a note and a tour schedule in the mail.

It was perfect timing. I had just got "let go" from my mind-numbing data entry job for reasons involving photocopiers and pornography when Guy from the band Fugazi sent me a tour schedule for the band's southern tour.

I hung out long enough to get my last paycheck, and with just a few hundred dollars in my pocket headed south to Atlanta, where Fugazi was to play two nights at a club called The Masquerade. I didn't have an address for the club or any idea where it was, so the first thing I did when I got to Atlanta was stop at a gas station and lock my keys in my car.

A voice said, "Hey, buddy."

I looked to see who it was. "How's it going?"

"Hey man, do you have a couple bucks you could buy us a pack of cigarettes with?" His girlfriend stood beside him.

"Cigarettes? Sorry man, you're on your own."

"Look, man," he persisted, "we don't need the cigarettes. We just want to empty the tobacco out and roll joints with them. You want some joints, man? I'll give you some joints if you buy us some cigarettes."

I had the feeling I was in a very bad neighborhood to be a

white boy from Ann Arbor.

Fortunately, I'm not really from Ann Arbor. "Look. I just locked my damn keys in my car."

"Oh, yeah? Which one's your car?"

"This one."

He looked in the window. "Yep. There they are. Right on the front seat." The keys lay in full view on the open atlas. "Well, I could get them out for you. I know how to do it."

"If you can get those keys out," without smashing my window, I thought to myself, "I'll buy you those cigarettes." This guy was either a dope-smoking car thief or a smooth-talker who could spot a sucker a mile away—or at least from the sidewalk of Amoco.

"Baby, go get me a coat hanger." His girlfriend left for a minute and came back with a coat hanger. Don't ask me from where. It took a while for it to sink into him that the Honda's locks were straight vertical slabs and cannot be hooked. Maybe he was just high. "My buddy's got a slim jim."

"Really?" *That's a handy tool for a dope-smoking car thief.*

"Yeah, man. He lives just around the corner. Walk me over to his house."

We walked around the corner. "If anybody asks, my name's Greg and you went to high school with me."

"It's great to see you again, Greg, old buddy." I shook his hand.

"Now my friend ain't gonna let us use his slim jim for free," said 'Greg'. "You got seven dollars?"

"Seven dollars?"

"Yeah, man. You got to pay the man to use his slim jim."

We were standing at a gate. Long apartments stretched back before us. My buddy 'Greg' was about to take my money and smoke a big crack rock in some roach-infested tenement. It sure was sad to see my old school chum turn out like this. I gave him the seven bucks and never saw him again.

I went back to the gas station, told the guy at the counter my situation, and asked to use a phone. In a thick accent he let me know there was nothing he could possibly do for me. Outside, I stared stupidly at the sky.

Someone else approached me. "Hey, buddy. I'm trying to get an ID, so I can get a job. Can you help me out with a dollar or two?"

"An ID?" *A fool and his money are soon targeted.*

"Yeah, an ID. A picture ID so I can get a job. I need some money to pay for it. Is that your car?"

"It sure is."

"Too bad about your keys." He looked at my plates. "You from Missouri?"

"No. I drove down from Michigan to see a show at the Masquerade. Ever heard of it?"

"The Masquerade? Yeah! Wait here a minute, and I'll tell you right where it is!" He ran off. He came back. "You're real close, man! It's right down the street."

"Down there?"

"Yeah!" He gestured down the street. "Right down there on the right."

"Wow! Thanks!" I gave him two bucks. "Hope you get that ID." *Or at least a cold 40 of Mickey's.*

He walked off. I stared stupidly at my car.

A man in a blue uniform came up to me. "You lock your key in car?" he asked in an accent either Indian or Arabic.

"I sure did."

"Here. I have slim jim in my truck." He took a slim jim from the back of his pickup and in one swift motion the door was open. "I work in parking garage. Have this problem all of time."

I couldn't believe it. "Thank you so much!"

"No problem. Bye now."

What luck! I hopped in my car and drove down the street to the Masquerade. The Masquerade is like Saint Andrew's in

Detroit in that it is multi-leveled for dancing and concerts, but it looks like the designers couldn't decide if they were building spooky apartments or a demented warehouse.

The concert hall is two or three stories above the ground. The bands load all their gear onto a platform that descends from where the upper level juts out over and away from the first level, above the parking lot and ticket-line entrance. I watched the opening band load up and rise into the air.

The show was sold out.

I hung out with some kids in the parking lot, the kind whose main fashion accessories are paint and safety pins. They didn't have tickets either and were wondering what to do and where one of the girls was going to stay now that she'd been kicked out of her father's house. They reminded me of some friends I had in high school. We joked that Ian MacKaye would be the hardest person to party with after the show.

"Hey, Ian, have a beer!"

"No!"

"Hey Ian, wanna hit this joint?"

"*No!*"

"Wanna get some groupie chicks?"

"I'VE GOT THE STRAIGHT EDGE!!!"

"Damn, dude..."

I went to the manager. "Hey, I drove all the way from Michigan to see Fugazi, and the show's sold out. Is there any way you can get me in?"

"You drove from *Michigan*?"

"Yeah. This is my favorite band *ever* and I gotta get in."

"I've been having trouble with the Fire Marshall, so I gotta be careful. There's these two girls from South Carolina who asked me first. I can't promise anything."

Dicked. I went and sat down with the punks.

"What'd he say?" they asked.

"No go. Something about the Fire Marshall, he said."

"Shit."

Just then a man walked up to us and asked how we were. "Does anybody want to buy a ticket?"

"A ticket?!? How much?!?"

"Six bucks."

I looked at my new friends.

"You better take it," they said. "We're all together anyway. You drove all the way from Michigan."

"I'll take it!" I fished the happiest six dollars that ever lived out of my pocket, said thanks, good-bye to the punks, and went inside.

I had a beer and watched the opening bands, then stood expectantly waiting for Fugazi. A girl who seemed to have taken large doses of LSD that night started rubbing my hair and stroking my beard. She did it to every guy in reach, playing with their hair.

I asked the guy she was with, "Is she always like this?"

"Pretty much."

"Hey!" I called to her. "Do you think you could get up to the front?" The crowd was tightly packed. Being a guy, I'd need to shove my way through. But with a girl...

"Sure! Wanna go up front?"

"Yes!"

She took my hand and navigated the sea of bodies. We were about three bodies from the stage. "How's this?"

"It's great!" I could've kissed her for it—but who was that guy she was with?

Then the band was on stage. The music started, and the girl and I got smashed forward. I think they started with *Public Witness Program* from *In on the Killtaker*, a driving number with a hard-core edge. The sea of bodies swelled up and down like waves with no shore on which to break but themselves.

Fugazi pounded out song after song, dedicating *Downed City* from *Red Medicine* to everyone in Atlanta who wasn't so happy about the Olympics coming to their town, the first line being "I want to go, I want to get out!" There were cheers of agreement.

Soon, I wandered out of the thick of it to watch and listen without being crushed. When the show was over I went up to guy in the Masquerade shirt on stage and, holding up my *13 Songs* CD said, "I drove all the way from Michigan to see these guys and I want them to sign my *13 Songs*!"

"You'll have to talk to the backstage guy."

"Where's he?"

"Around that side. You'll see him."

I went around. I saw him. "Hey! I drove all the way from Michigan to see these guys and I want to get them to sign my CD!"

Without a word he grabbed me by the shoulders and set me down a long hallway behind the stage.

I ran just a few steps then turned back to him. "But where are they?"

He pointed. "Back there!"

"Okay!" I ran down the hall.

Backstage, the bass player Joe sat on a couch with some of the opening band. Alcohol was conspicuously absent, replaced with bottled water and Perrier. First Joe signed my CD booklet, then Brendan. Then Guy came through and signed.

Then Ian MacKaye descended the stairs.

I met Ian once before with my friend Dan as we sat outside waiting for a show in Missouri. We were 18 and worshipped the guy. He passed by us and said, "What's up, fellas?"

We were like, "Hey, not much," and he walked on. We turned to each other.

"Matthew... was that..."

"Dan... I think that was..."

Then together: "Oh, shit! That was Ian MacKaye!"

I hoped this encounter would be a little more intelligent. He found a pen and sat beside me.

I asked him, "Did you get the Christmas card I sent you? The one with the angel on front playing the guitar?"

He looked at me. "That was you? What's your name?"

"I'm Matthew from Ann Arbor!"

He looked at me even harder. "Let me see your driver's license."

What? That was the last thing I had expected to hear. Was I really getting carded by Ian MacKaye?

I handed over my license. "It's from Washington. I lived there for a while."

He handed it back. "What are you doing here?"

Everybody now! "I drove all the way from Michigan to see you guys! I'm going to follow you as long as my money and car hold out!"

He took out a little black book. "That's your own shit, but as long as you do it, I'll put you on the guest list. Just come back and see me after each show and I'll put you on for the next one." He wrote my name.

"Wow! Thanks!"

He signed my CD booklet in his trademark block-letter signature—IAN—and took off.

A girl behind me said, "Hey! You're the guy from Michigan!"

I turned around. Two girls shared a large chair behind me. "How do you know that?" *And how did I get a reputation here already?*

"The manager told us about you!"

Here they were: the two girls from South Carolina the manager had mentioned. We got to talking and went out for a snack at the IHOP down the street. By the end of the meal I had been talked into following them back to South Carolina. They were going to show me around Charleston and give me a place to sleep.

And that's exactly what happened.

31

Unfortunately, my car's left front C-V joint started going bad, so after a day in Charleston I drove down to see Fugazi in Savannah where they played a totally different set, including all the songs I had wished for but didn't hear in Atlanta, like *Birthday Pony* and *Repeater*.

Ian detests the slam-dancing that seems to prevail at their shows. It seems inevitable to me, given the high-energy-high-anger-fuck-you of the music, but that's how he sees it. And you know, it is cool to see a show without some idiot kicking you in the mouth. The rest of the band remains silent on the issue.

After a particularly scathing indictment of the slam crowd, the band started into *Waiting Room* which begins, breaks for seven beats, then kicks in with the drums on the eighth beat and takes off again. At the break, Ian interjected, "That guy Ian is such a *dick!*" Boom boom boom boom boom BAM! Back into the song. *Damn, I love this band.*

After another great show, I realized I needed to drive home and see about getting my car fixed. I was just about out of cash. I headed up to the stage and reached out my hand to Guy. He shook it. I yelled, "You guys are STILL the greatest!" and got back on the road.

Michigan Again

July 12, 1999. Club Heidelberg.

Erin takes the microphone into the crowd singing, "You're the ugliest thing I ever seen - but I think I love you, honey!" Her girls, a crowd of dykes called the Burly Girlies, sing along, shouting their approval and undulating as a single organism. Matt and Barrett drive the grinding, heavy riff of the tune inexorably forward like a rhinoceros in heat. The hall is packed with friends and strangers, pitchers of beer and packs of cigarettes. Wailing notes hang in the air, floating above the space, before strafing the crowd. This may be the best night of my life. It is a good thing I love every second of it, because it is the last time I will ever play with these guys.

Erin, a gruff, macho dyke with a rock and roll chip on her shoulder put this band together. You either loved her or hated her. Her room was a shrine to her rock icons. Elvis Presley and Janis Joplin partied on the walls with Joan Jett, L7, and the Lunachicks. In one corner she kept her Gibson SG. I played it for ten minutes before she asked me to take the lead guitar slot. I had an SG, too. I accepted without a second's hesitation.

In the short space of a few months, we became best friends. Every Tuesday, we played together, sharing ideas and creating new ones. She asked me to teach her things on the guitar, absorbing my hand-written notes like a sponge. Within a few years, she transformed from a girl who didn't know how to play a single chord to a rock-solid guitarist who tore off Iron Maiden songs note for note, eventually surpassing me in her knowledge of metal.

In return, Erin fed me. "Cutie Pie!" She'd call out when I walked into her hot dog joint. "Rock Dog!" She wrote Cutie Pie on my orders so the staff would call it out when my food came up, and she would crack up. Living hand to mouth at various temp jobs, I welcomed the chance to eat like a pig that summer: plates of onion rings and waffle fries smothered in melted cheese and topped with chili. The scent of grilled meat and deep fryers still smells like somebody loves me. We drank Jack Daniels out of black flasks and kicked up our Harley Davidson-shod feet on the table to listen to Danzig's first album. We rapped about our psycho girlfriends and laughed at dirty jokes together. Erin's brother Barrett eventually filled the drum chair for us and his friend Matt took over the low-end on bass.

We rocked in the face of oppression. The University denied

us electricity at our outdoor show on campus. When we pirated the juice from a distant outlet, they sent security to shut us down. We opened a show at a bar, and the headliners were so blown away with the crowd we brought in that they gave us half their take. We went to Detroit and played a ripping set for which a walloping five people showed up. But that didn't stop us. We were too far into it. The energy was too intense. Everything we achieved together brought us closer together personally and musically. Energy builds up in a band like that. The best takes of a song, the best improvisations, have a sexual element to their energy as you create something new together and pump it full of life. You pour yourself into it.

When we hit the studio, we faced one problem after another. Barrett and Matt were very sick. The guy didn't have all the tapes we needed, and when I drove quite some distance to buy them, my thermostat went south, dangerously overheating the engine. The store wasn't even open yet!

But, by the time I got back, I didn't care. I loved that band, and I knew we could smoke that recording session if we could just keep going. There was no frustration that could stop the inevitable. Perry Farrell of Jane's Addiction sang, "Keep it up. You'll be born." It was never more true for me than on that day. That session, despite the obstacles—or maybe because of them—captured the tightest, most intense performances we ever pulled off. It was worth every second.

I once had a dream about being on stage with Mudhoney. In the dream, my guitar solo hit the perfect note. It's hard to explain what that means, but it was just the most powerful note ever played. I never felt like that in real life until I played with those guys.

Erin booked a gig following those sessions. She gave her usual gruffly nonchalant introduction along the lines of, "Uh, hey, we're Down and Dirty and thanks for coming." A fireworks finale went off in my head, and I realized Barrett was hammering out the most aggressive version of our opening tune he ever played. Relentless. Uncompromising. Euphoric. He played like it was his last night on Earth.

It wasn't—but it *was* the last time we would ever play together. While I thought it was just the beginning, Erin and Barrett's personal concerns brought the band to an abrupt, unannounced halt. Show's over, folks.

These days, when I find a truly awesome collaborator, I savor every second we play together. When I find something that excites me, I throw myself into it. When I have a chance to unleash my creative energy, I do it whole-heartedly. Don't hold back. You never know if this time could be the last.

NINE

DREAMS

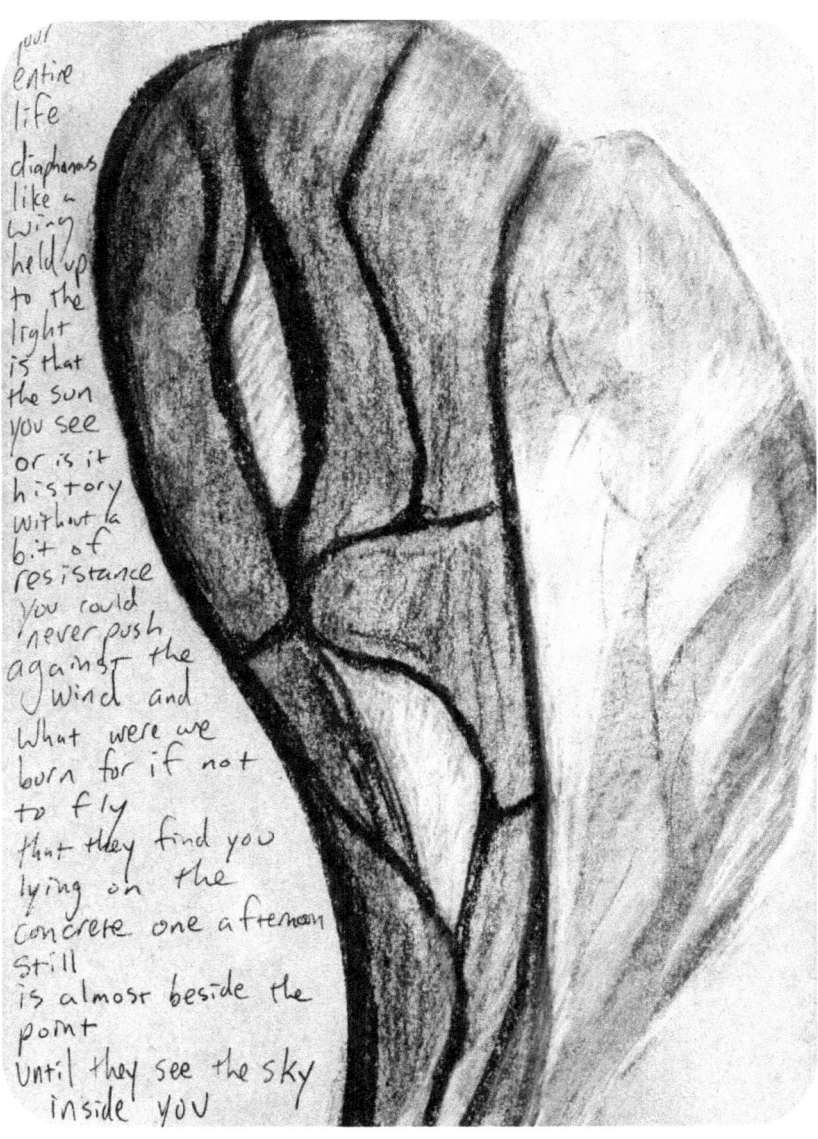

your
entire
life
diaphanous
like a
wing
held up
to the
light
is that
the sun
you see
or is it
history
without a
bit of
resistance
you could
never push
against the
wind and
what were we
born for if not
to fly
that they find you
lying on the
concrete one afternoon
still
is almost beside the
point
until they see the sky
inside you

Campus Sequence

You and your buddy, as played by Ben Affleck, uncover a conspiracy. Walking down white hallways with grey marble tile floors, you discuss your options. The blurry background of a photograph provides a clue: the lockers.

You and Ben find the lockers, opening all of them, not exactly sure what you are looking for. Ben figures it out. One locker has a small magnet on the inside door: a round black magnet encased in some protective layer, a waxy substance you might expect to find on a circuit board component.

Ben is certain this is what you need. Although you don't discuss the details, your mind races to fill in an explanation for the magnet. Probably, you think, it contains encrypted data that will bring this whole conspiracy down.

The afternoon light is fading to dusk. You head back down the hallway where Ben dashes up a flight of stairs and disappears. You try to follow him. The white stairs make a narrow spiral leading to a small hole in the ceiling.

How did he get through there? You try to squeeze through without falling off the tiny stairs or losing the magnet. The narrow opening pins your arms to your side.

On the other side of the hole, you emerge slowly and uncomfortably through the floor of a second level. The room is a cross between a library and a control room from a science fiction movie, a command and information center lit by dozens of screens and thousands of tiny lights.

Three men sit at desks in a central station, watching you conspicuously emerge from the floor. You joke about how you hope you don't hurt yourself, trying to look like a regular guy having a problem instead of someone suspicious. They don't seem happy, but they make no move to stop you.

But you and Ben are discovered. You are in danger now. The two of you go back to the lower hallway as the twilight fades further into night. Soldiers are coming.

You run down the hallway and find a side door that branches off in two directions. Ben takes the left and disappears into darkness. You take the right and end up in some kind of bathroom or mop room. It's hard to tell in the dark grey light. Everything is the same dark grey color.

After a short time of silence, you can't resist the urge to peek out and see if the coast is clear. Slowly you advance out of the room, moving towards the hallway hesitantly. Something or someone slams into you. You can't see who it is, but it scares the hell out of you. It's the last thing you remember.

You wake up. Who was it, and what happened next? Going back to sleep, you try to resume the dream only to find out it was an episode, like a TV show, centered around the campus-like setting. The next episode begins, picking up in a different place with a different story, leaving the mystery unsolved.

✳

Hotel Sequence

Someone stole the steak. That wasn't right. First, it arrived in glistening plastic wrap with a plate full of food. And then? It vanished.

It seems par for the course in this crappy hotel room. It has a cubby hole in the vaulted wall and double desk crammed into the space. After the bed, there isn't much space left over.

You have to laugh. The hotel, quaintly picturesque from the outside, reveals this crappy old room again. But it's not a totally bad room. You can live with it for a little bit.

Check this out. You've got a roommate. Maybe he stole the steak. Maybe it was Liz at the foot of the stairs, who discussed computers enthusiastically with you. But no, she seemed genuinely interested, and the entire party in the ballroom downstairs was quite supportive.

Then you see her picture. This girl you knew… when? It was the last time you were here. You'd forgotten it, like a dream. But it comes back to you now. You said goodbye to her on the balcony of the hotel. You loved her then, and you love dreaming her memory now from this photo.

You couldn't help but leave her, and it was okay. It had something to do with the atomic bomb you worked on, living in this coastal paradise, enjoying the weather, building the bomb with the professor and the genius. Times were simpler then, in the days of the bomb.

But that was years ago, back when you and Joe Pesci stopped in the street to discuss his newspaper: a touching moment. Or the time you and Dave joked about the Presidio but you were nowhere near. And the car disappeared, but you carried on piggyback. Those were good times.

This hotel. It's different from the house. The house has hidden levels, too. Places you have trouble finding again. You find a door to it from somewhere else every now and then, from another location you discover which has a connection to a distant room in the house. Sometimes you only realize later that two unrelated settings are connected by doorways to the house.

Sometimes you find yourself in a room in the house for which you can find no door. You know you're in the house, but you can't get clear on how the room connects to anything else.

The door in the fire room leads downstairs through a claustrophobic's nightmare, but the walls don't close in. They lead to the basement. It's hidden, but you get there more than once. It's just the strange location, the out of the way spot, the featureless hallway with the closet door that masks the fire room.

Surgical Sequence & Fun House

They remove the skin from your right forearm in surgery, then put it back on. They don't sew it back. They just put it there in the right place. They say not to worry about it.

Right. It feels like the pieces of skin are ready to separate and detach every time you move. "Don't worry about it," they tell you.

Finally, someone in a white coat comes to put a layer of brown, stretchy adhesive on your hand. They don't coat the whole arm, but at least it feels a little better.

The next night you're at the fun house. The fun house is named after the Stooges album. More rooms than you can count pile into the air, becoming tree houses at the very top. It's a fun place to hang out, the fun house—so much so that you have a room there.

In the room across the hallway, a half dozen or so people in various stages of undress share one king-size bed. The door is slightly open. The sun shines into the room. Guys and girls nap the mid-morning away. You see an old high school friend has joined their cuddle party.

Your lover joins you in your room. She's beautiful. So sad, so beautiful at the same time.

Concert Sequence

The two of you make love in the middle of the afternoon. You go for a drive beside the bay. Water and skyscrapers reflect the sun and sky. It's a beautiful day. She pretends the things you say don't hurt her.

Or maybe they just don't. You two drive together a lot lately. Just a couple of nights ago, she was in the driver's seat.

Derek Trucks plays at this club tonight. He sounds great. How does he get all that sound and speed with a slide? Hundreds of people fill long rows of folding chairs on the dancefloor and on bleachers.

You take out the Little Martin and play along. Derek has a three-chord jam going with the band, three major chords hitting B-flat, C, and D. It's fun, playing along with Derek. You pay attention now to remember the chords when you wake up.

The little kid in front of you turns around to tell you, "A security guard is coming this way." The kid makes it sound like you are busted for the acoustic jam.

But you look up, and a lot of people are heading for the emergency exit. Somebody might have tripped a silent fire alarm? Security staff helps everyone move out calmly, quietly.

You could say Derek Trucks was on fire tonight.

✳

Crime Scene

Chad takes you to Tim's house. You don't know Tim, but Chad says he's going to kill him. The house is empty on the first floor. In the kitchen, you watch as Chad loads a rifle and walks up the stairs to Tim's room.

When he comes back, you both leave the house and go for a long journey through rivers and forests. The landscape is unknown but familiar. Have you been here before? You find two vehicles and take them separately to Tim's house again. Why does Chad think this is a good idea?

You get there first and busy yourself wiping down the entire kitchen to erase any fingerprints. You know when the cops find Tim's body, they will be looking for evidence. You wipe the countertops. You wipe the cupboards.

Tim's family comes home and finds you cleaning. The

people are his mother, perhaps, and his grandmother. You calmly introduce yourself as a friend of Chad's who is, you say, on his way to visit their son. "What's your son's name?" you ask, as if you don't know.

"Tim," says one of the ladies.

"Right! Tim." You talk to them for a little while, all the while growing increasingly concerned you will be the prime suspect when they find Tim's dead body upstairs. But they never go up the stairs. Finally, Chad shows up acting like nothing happened, and you leave.

Your painting van is outside, but Chad has installed a sophisticated surveillance system inside it. You can see inside the house and monitor all the activity. You can even see into the basement. You can see everything in the house. It is winter.

✻

Joy Ride

You stand up in your car to take a shower as it races down the highway. You feel total confidence in your car's alignment, making only minor corrections to maintain your lane as you bathe. Other drivers turn to stare, watching you bathe through the walls of your car.

A long curve looms on the horizon, so you put both hands on the wheel. Cop cars and lights create a confusing flow of traffic. Off to the side, people shoot a movie. Past them, you turn left—straight into oncoming traffic!

Did you take the wrong turn? Are you going the wrong way? You can't be. You can clearly read the signs. Maybe it wasn't a wrong turn, but you are certainly going against the flow of traffic! You see an exit on the right.

Now it's all under control. Don't be nervous about the cops. You rocket off the exit ramp, unable to hold the turn, and fly off the road, through the air, as your car turns into a rubber boogie board.

You hit the rocks and pavement on your belly on the boogie board. Escaping injury, you start ground surfing. It's the cutting edge of a whole new sport! It's wildly fun!

Up and down, all around, circling the buildings and parking lots, performing wild stunts, you catch the attention of onlookers. You zoom off the pavement into suburban yards, coming to rest on someone's lawn.

Eye-level with the grass, you find yourself staring at a kid's ID standing up between the blades. Is the kid dead? Is this his lawn? Did his parents put this here as a memorial?

✳

Day Job

You have a ground-level apartment and a dog to take care of. It seems like too much to handle, this dog, and you don't want to do it. Then you remember you took care of her before, and everything is ok.

Your girlfriend comes over. You have two beds. The second one is too small, so you put both of the beds together: just right.

You go get a job. Shortly, you get a call from one of the guys at work. He has season tickets for the Cardinals and wants you to take them off his hands. The two of you have a great chat as you talk about this new job. You are laughing at how easy it is, and how it's totally cool to talk right now—and the phone is ripped out of your hands.

You are fired on the spot. "You are taking a personal call and telling them how dead it is right now!" they say. But there is something they are not telling you. You suspect you are being fired for daring to enjoy yourself and have fun. You suspect you are being fired for having no fear of being fired.

The manager pulls a bottle of red liquid out of your desk. Are they really firing you for having booze at work? It's not even booze. It's the red mix for margaritas. But they won't listen.

You decide to go to their other office, a bar/restaurant in Tempe. Standing around in your bathrobe, you chat with two of the waitresses. They say you have dried semen on the back of your robe. You say, "So what?" and you all laugh about it.

Then you find the guys in charge, the guys behind your getting fired. They give you a ration of bullshit. But one of them turns out to be a girl you went to school with. You put your arm around her and call her your old school chum. You used to have a massive crush on her.

The two of you go outside to sit. She says, "Now they won't have to call the cops to get you to leave. And, you know, I really wanted to talk to you about something." She begins to bare her soul. Her eyes go misty. Looking at her face, you realize just how damned gorgeous she is.

You wake up with her face fresh in your mind seconds before the alarm goes off.

✴

The Rescue

In the ruins of a city under siege, you produce a dimensional gateway. Everyone passes through it to escape to another city. You stand outside of a school in the pouring rain as daylight comes. People pass by carrying the wounded in stretchers.

You did it. You saved them all.

✴

The Journey

Despite the darkness, you can see all the walls and all the people are shades of ash grey. Winged people or perhaps demons fly through the air. Others scale the walls. The ceiling, several stories high, caps a vast concert hall. You've been here before, but not for many years. You once saw your favorite band here. The only light comes from black lights.

The concert turns out to be political speeches. You accept a mission to go down front to the stage and get a recorded interview and close-up pictures of the speakers. Among them is Barack Obama with suits and security everywhere. You have no trouble getting close to the stage because you know someone up there.

You travel a maze of hallways lit like daytime in schools and offices. You end up on a ship and decide to take a voyage on a strange craft. It consists of a metal dome atop a floating rubber ring. It will be a difficult and solitary journey to get back to land.

You lose control of the vessel and lose all outside communication. The vessel is sturdy and seaworthy, but do you even know where you are? Will you have enough food? If you get lost, how will anyone find you?

After a great storm, you land on a beach. You stand outside your vessel, safe and sound. In the distance, a large metal warship floats below a plane in the sky. You think of your best friend. Isn't he supposed to meet you here?

You look around and realize what a gorgeous day it is. The sun shines over a stunningly beautiful sea.

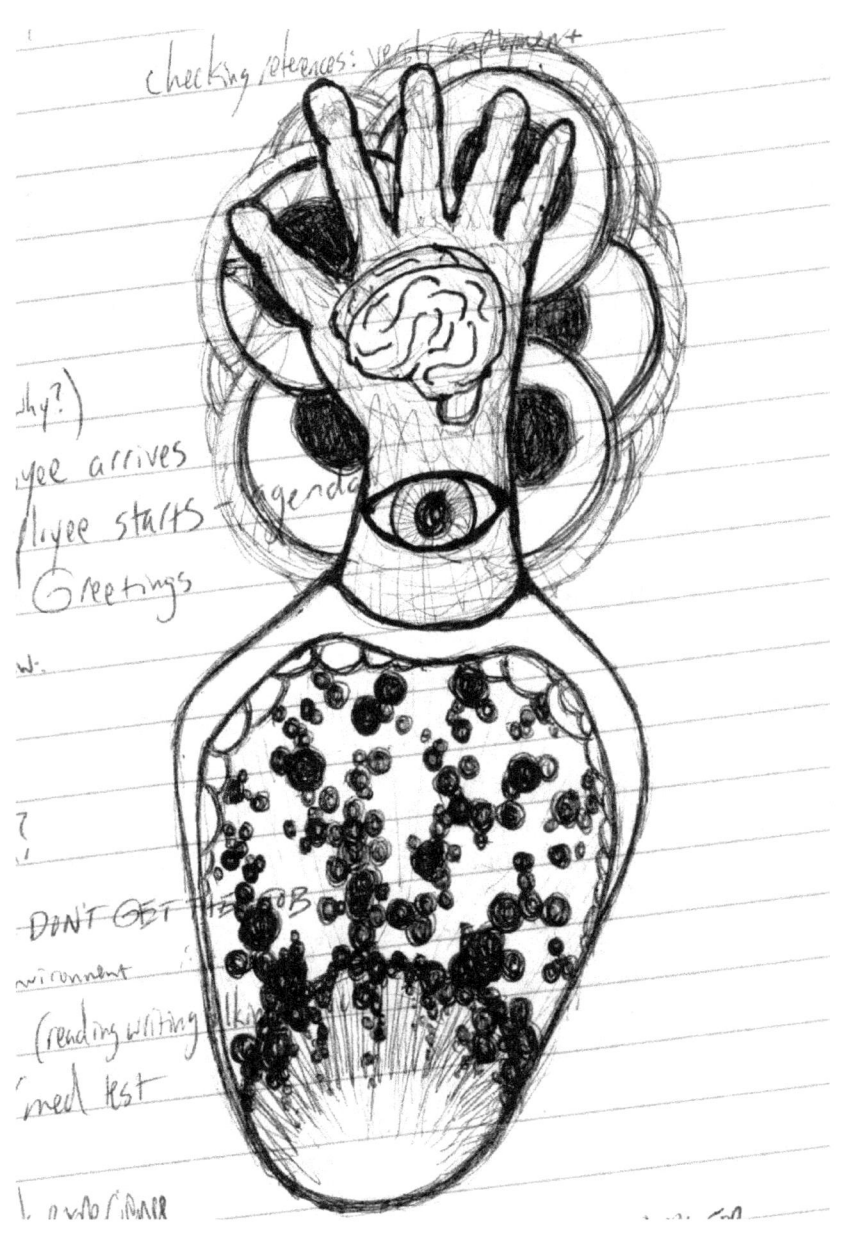

FOURTEEN
SKETCHES

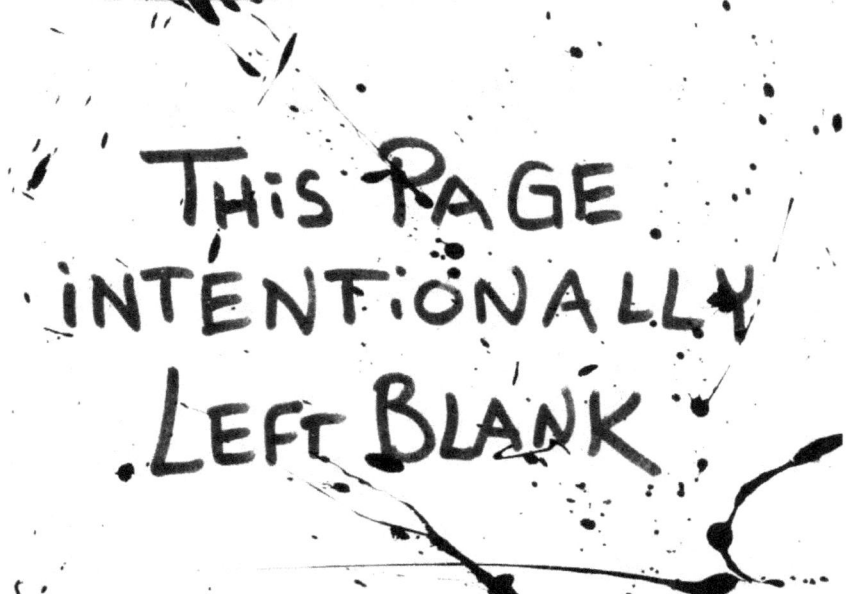

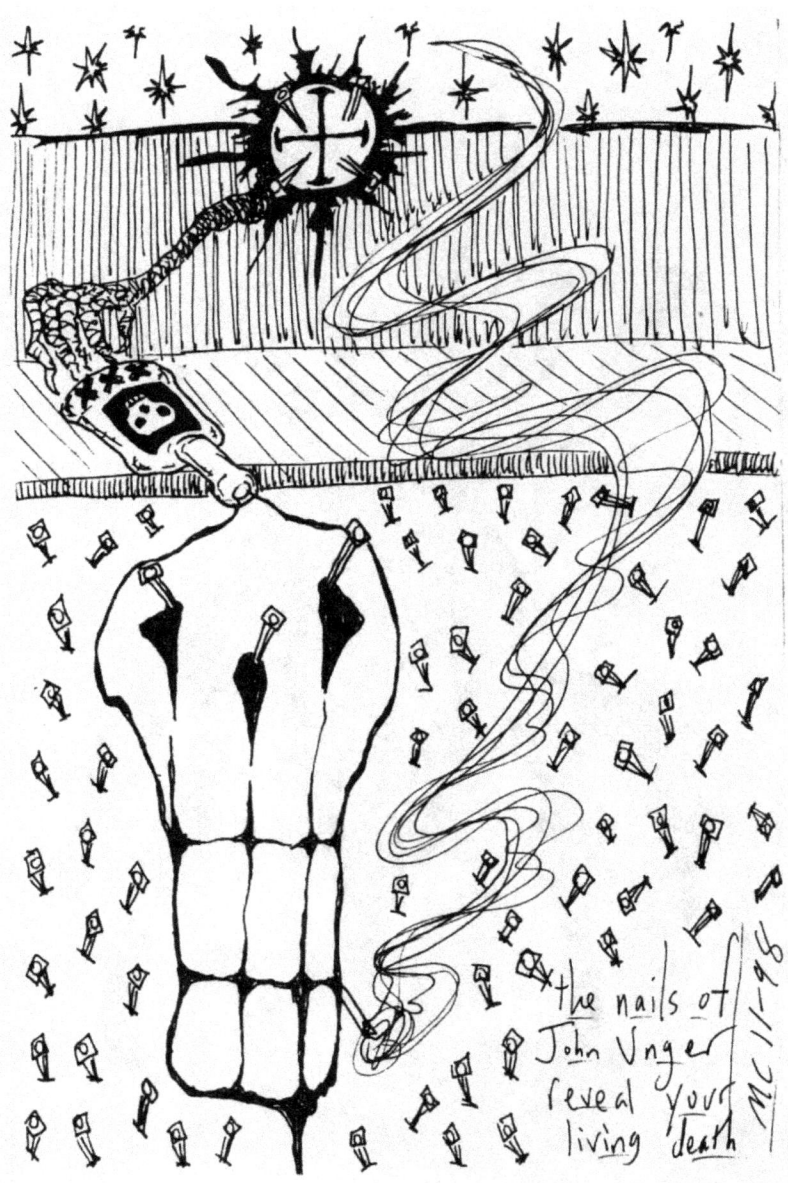

the nails of
John Unger
reveal your
living death

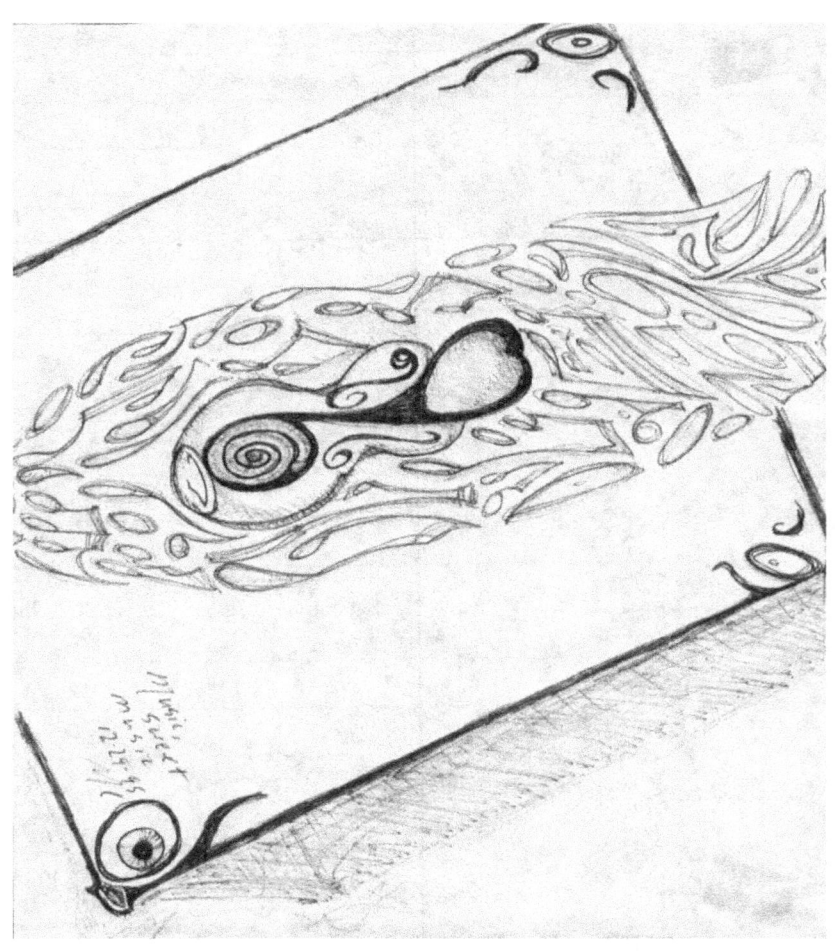

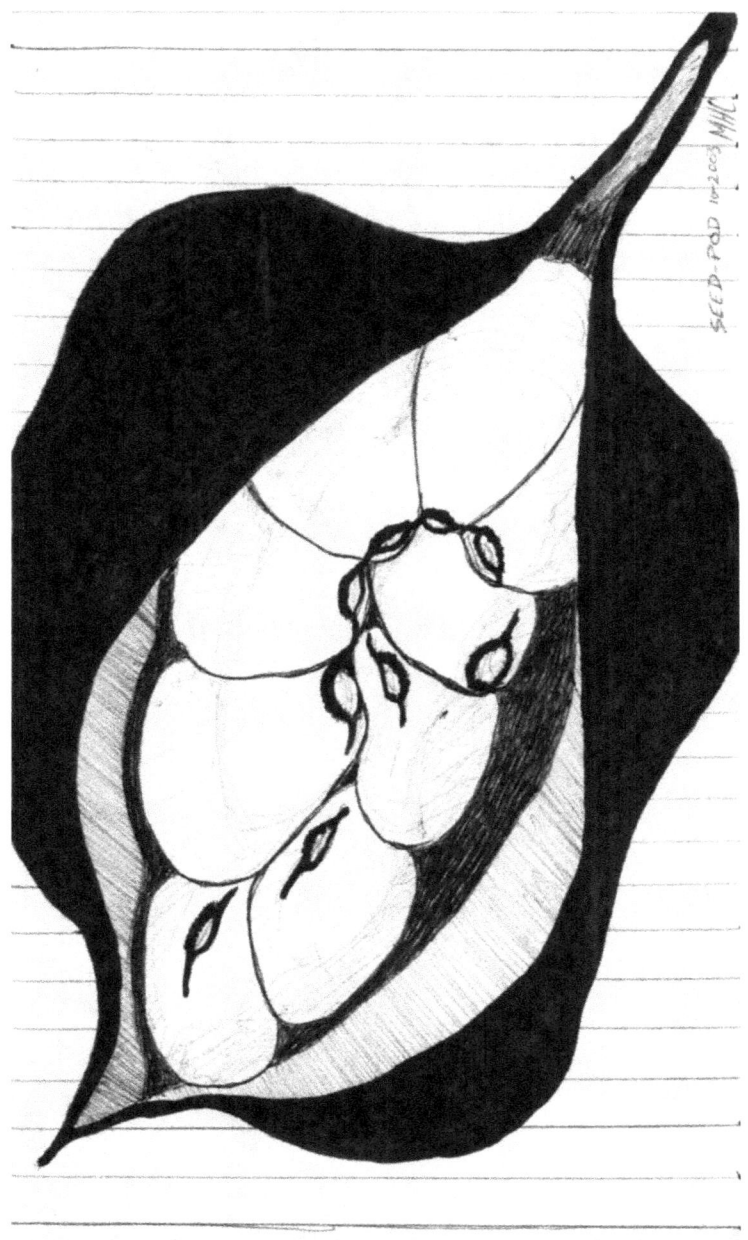

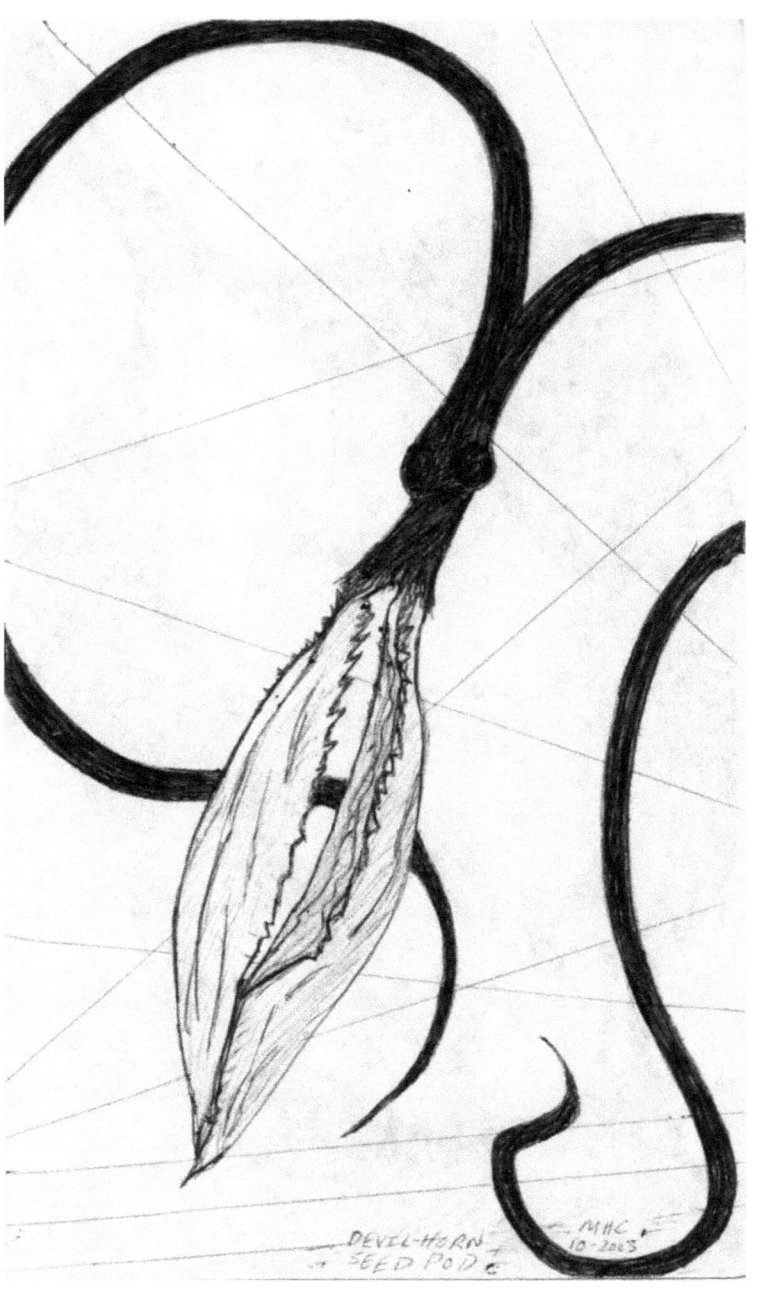

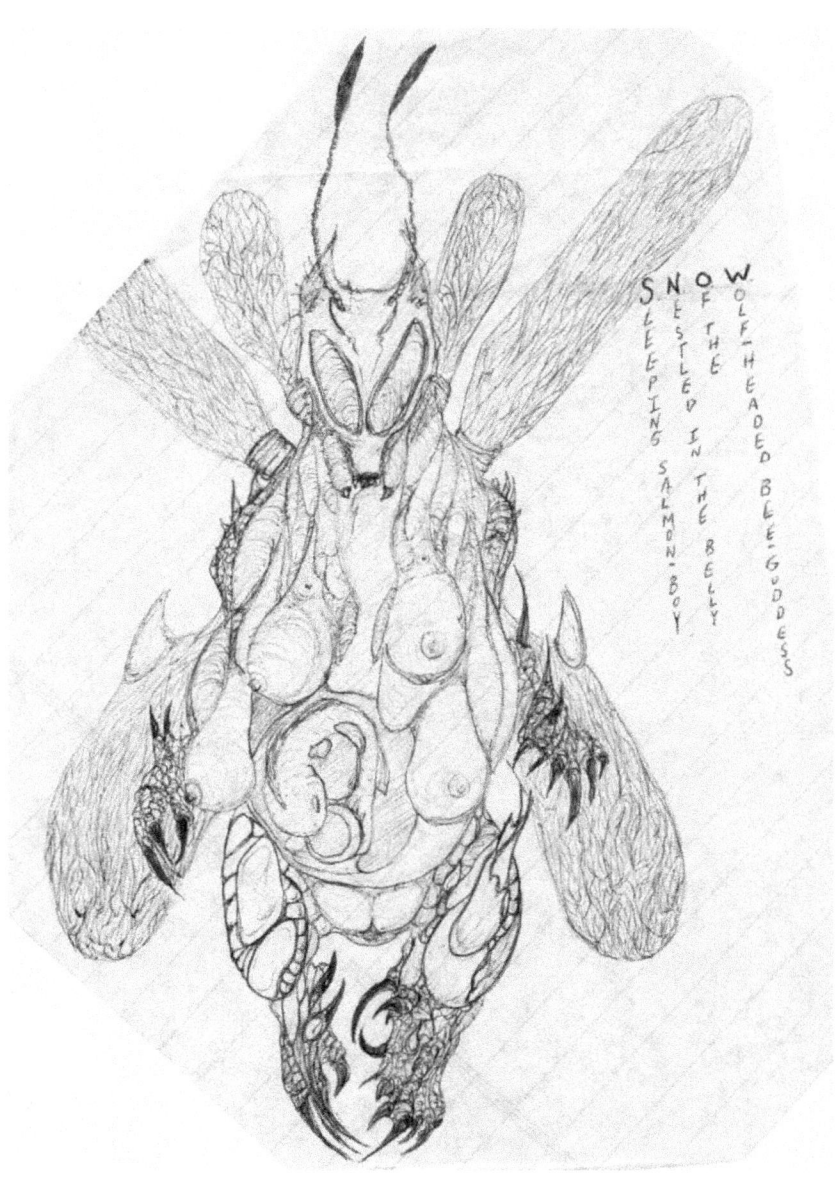

SNOW
OF THE
SLEEPING SALMON-BOY
NESTLED IN THE BELLY
WOLF-HEADED BEE-GODDESS

She is a tree of fire whose branches reach out to embrace the sky and whose roots reach deep down into the Earth where they take hold and draw up the energy of life into her fire

MHC 2002

THIRTY
SONGS

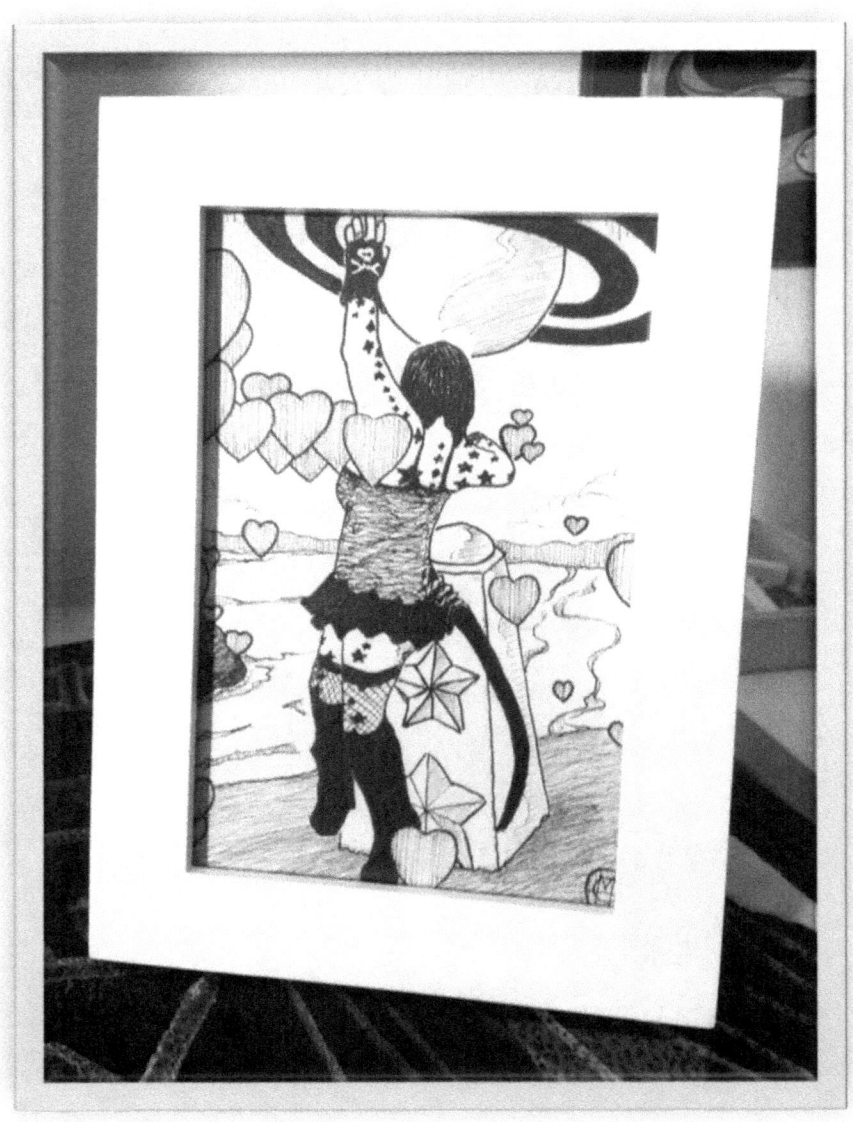

YOU KILL TIME
San Diego CA 1999

Said he'd always manage to kill time
Or at least to make it beg for mercy
Stretch it out 'til it's all full of holes
And step on through tomorrow

Flower never wilts
Machine never rusts
Body never ages
Never turns to dust

How he loves his alchemy
The secrets never, no they never lie
He takes his lead and turns it into gold
And he keeps on killin' time until it dies

Flower never wilts
Machine never rusts
Body never ages
Never turns to dust

WENT SOUTH
Ann Arbor MI 2002

Did she paint for you a picture?
Was it so pretty you could cry?
When the walls come down
Do you ever wonder why?

Did you sign your name in blood?
Did that last as long as ink?
Does anybody tell the truth ?
Now what the hell do you think?

I know it's all been said before
I know that I should shut my mouth
It would not bother me
If this whole damn thing went south
I wouldn't care at all

Was the scene set so perfect
That you made yourself at home?
Then you're out on the streets
And they batter your body with stones

You know the right way to start up your day
Take all your feelings and lock them away
Send them to me C.O.D. someday
And I'll keep them safe at home
You know you're not alone

BALLAD OF A BAD COYOTE
Ann Arbor MI 2001

Lie on that steel there, babe. Let me draw a line
The man who makes his bed of nails hopes to lie
Lie in it, lay in it, or get laid in it - whatever
I got a thing for a girl who does this thing with fire

Sex and Death are great but the sex comes first
Sometimes it's dangerous, you know sometimes it hurts
I don't mind the cost, baby, I don't mind the pain
I just want to see your body in a haze of flame

Go to the light
Then turn right
Everybody needs a head on a platter
Once in their life

Old Scratch says, man, he says, hey, I'm a bad coyot'
Scratch that, man, he says, I'm a great coyot'
The problem is, it seems, I'm a goddamn rotten human being
I did it with a married woman and I'd do it all again

Party down
Party on down
If you can't pay the bills
Get drunk with the hounds

If you get them drunk enough
They lose your trail

ACCIDENTAL PERFECTION

San Diego CA 1999

Isolate the colors
And you rob them of their light
Isolate the stars and wonder
Why they burn out of the sky

I wouldn't lie to you
Wouldn't tell you things you want to hear
I wouldn't lie to you
I'm trying to make it all come clear

Isolate the candle
We can burn it at both ends
Meet me in the middle, boy
I swear that's where the fun begins

I wouldn't lie to you
Wouldn't tell you things you want to hear
I wouldn't lie to you
I'm trying to make it all come clear

Shine a little light into
The corners of your soul
Accidental perfection, and then
It's time to go

LUCKY SEVEN
Ann Arbor MI 2001

You know all those things we couldn't live without?
None of it means a damn thing to me now:

The third world war, the people next door
Your little scraps of paper all over the floor
The outside world, the boys and girls
Let 'em all go hang, let 'em all go hang

I used to think if I could think enough
Then I'd clear this whole thing up
But what I feel man, you know it don't make any sense
It don't recognize no consequence

I don't care, I don't see
I don't give a damn what comes to me
You're my drug, you're my rush
You're the one I want too much

If I roll my lucky number seven
If I die and I make it up to heaven
If it turns out they'll give me what I want
There's only one thing
Only one thing
Only one

TAYLOR'S BRIDGE

Ann Arbor MI 1997

Though we've built some bridges now
Close my eyes and I still see
Your shadow faces coming out
They are etched forever in my memory

We were torn out at the seams
Something slips right through the cracks and falls into my dreams
You can send me pictures, glorify your smile
I still trace the tears that washed away the miles

On we go from day to day
Yes, I chose to go – was suicide to stay
Though your picture lights up my day
I have to put you down and turn my head away

I forgive you now
Though not about to forget
I was just caught out in your storm
I was all soaking wet

That blade of ice caught in your eye
It marks the look I know could kill
And though you pray we'll never die
I know that someday I will

DEMOLITION

Ann Arbor MI 2002

You got a bulldozer for a brain
You got a jackhammer in your skull
It's like staring down the business end of
A wrecking ball

If you choose to go insane
That's just checking out the easy way
Your city crumbles into ashes
Broken glass and disarray

You better find yourself a hole
Crawl inside and hide your face
The men in hard hats, oh, they come tomorrow
To take your shit and haul it away

A demolition

GLITTER
Ann Arbor MI 1997

Half of you is a mirror
Half of you is all broken glass
Half of you is a hammer
Take a swing - don't wait to ask

Mother mother feed me
When my mouth falls open
Lying cracked and bleeding
Fix me when I am broken

Sell your ideals on a hope for change, but
Why do all the pennies rust?
Why do the dreams all fade?
Because they must

A BIT LIKE GOD
San Diego CA 2000

You must have felt a bit like god
Close the switch and light the sky
How the towers rise

You must have known no woman's touch
Could cut so deep or last so long
Lightning sang for you her song

What you found you'd give to all
Hate to tell you but your dream must fall
Without wires they'd have no thralls

Maybe the signal that you sent was strong
Enough to pick it up as time rolled on
I'll send you one that will never be gone

A bit like god,
Lightning sang for you her song

DANDELION
Ann Arbor MI 2002

Dandelion
You'll try anything
If I'm lying
It don't mean a thing
Where you going
Far away from home
But it sure beats being alone

You were barefoot
Laughing in the rain
When I saw you
Now I'll never be the same
Where you going
Correct me if I'm wrong
But you're still out singing your song

Everybody tries
To understand your life
If they say you're wrong
You just keep on singing your song

MORNING SONG
Ann Arbor MI 2002

Hey girl
Don't mind your scars
Carved on your arms
Wear them with pride for me

Hey girl
Don't mind the rain
It goes away
Won't be that long from now

If you
Don't mind routine
Or loud machinery
We've got a job for you

If you
Can't take the heat
You'll end on the streets
And we know where that gets you

Hey girl
I know it's cliché
Follow your heart away
Don't stick around for this

Hey babe
I'll be with you soon
Just close your eyes
Won't be too long from now

TANTRIC LOVE SONG
Ann Arbor MI 2002

I offer up this body to you
Do anything that you want to
You know you're the honey on my tongue
Don't make me wait so long

Now you're into something new
Tell me what you want to try - be true
You're my little gift from the heavens above
Thrill me with your love

What I want from you
Is every, everything you do

CUT TOO DEEP
Phoenix AZ 2003

What you needed to live, it brings you down
I can't see any reason to keep it around
You collect bad habits like some people collect shit for their shelves
I can't sit by and watch you while you cut yourself

You hold your life in your hands, now you throw it away
I'm here to take it all back, I want you to stay
I can say this because I know just what you're doing too well
I can't sit by and watch it while you cut yourself

Stop yourself
Before you cut too deep

ONE DROP OF BLOOD
Olympia WA 1994

No one ever made a bed
I could lie in very well
Don't you think I realize
I put the ones I love through hell?

Now I know I made this bed
I grow tired of this stone beneath my head
Come on down from heaven, angel
I'll build the altar if you care to tangle

One drop of blood
You tasted freedom in our love
I can't help the way I feel
Can't you tell which lies are real?

FACE DOWN
Phoenix AZ 2002

I fell face down into drifts of white
I can't recall where I am tonight
I was on my way out to your place
Hoping that I'd find some kind of comfort there

Alcoholic dreams burn with a certain light
They can make you blind, oh they glitter and they shine
I lie here in the snow, peaceful, unaware
Try to wake me up – see if I care

Somebody wake me up
Rescue me tonight
Somebody call my name
Before the light that lives inside me dies

The thought of you with another man
Drives me to the edge. Can't you understand?
So I lose my mind, hurt others, hurt myself
Then I crawl right back after pissing in the well

Circles spin around. Time comes to an end.
Longing for the charms of my only friend
Lying in this cell, I've had lots of time to think
The first thing that I'll do when I get out of here is drink

WILD ABANDON
Phoenix AZ 2002

They told her she was a fool to leave the safety she'd become
They warned her off of the edge, said she'd unravel and then some
But have you seen the light that's in her eyes?
Live and love your life with wild abandon

Standing up on the stage, watch her blow all the lights out
She's got the words and the rage to blow all their minds now
He's fascinated by the way that she moves
How she came into being on a wave of a perfect light

She went with him for a ride – it makes a hell of a story
She tasted agony sweet, felt the pain and the glory
She's fascinated by the fact that her dreams
Will allow her to fly but it's gone when she opens her eyes

Lying in the middle of the crater fascinated by the impact
Once you hit the earth like that, there's just no way to turn back
He's fascinated by the songs of the birds
How they wade in the tide on the edge of a moonlit night

ALWAYS ROOM FOR ONE MORE
San Diego CA 2001

Hey boy you can sell yourself to power
Sell them on a line you wrote yourself
Stop at the tool booth, they always say you're welcome
There's always room for one more soul in hell

Thanks for taking me to see your buried treasure
Thanks for showing me where the diamonds lie
Would you like to come and see my prize possession
You can look into my heart if you desire

Come tell me boy just what you think might happen
When you finally catch that star you chase
What would happen if you caught that light tomorrow
Can you imagine what will be on that sweet day

LAST CALL
Las Vegas NV 2003

The broken bulb in my hand, the strangers in my bed
I got a line to my nose shooting straight to my head
Sometimes I gotta trash my place just to see where I live
I got a line on a guy who was nailed to forgive

Waiting for the last call
Last call never comes

If you've got a minute I'll admit it's just a flip of the coin
Heads I'm going to Vegas but tails it was New Orleans
Sometimes I wake in Vegas and wonder, hey man what the fuck?
Trying to chase a dream in a city built on my bad luck

I should have moved to a town where all of the bars close
That's the time of the night when you find someone to take home
But all you get in Vegas is wasted, broke and alone

SWEET DELILAH
San Diego CA 1999

Sweet Delilah, take what's yours
Let the rivers run their course, Delilah

Sweet Delilah, take what's mine
Everything grows back with time, Delilah
Like a flame on a fox-tail ride

Break my body
On your wheel
Take my eyes
But I can steal you blind
Like a flame on a fox-tail ride

HIWAY 80
Ann Arbor MI 2002

The only thing that holds me now
Is the dream of being lost again
Lost and dancin' over snake a-twistin' hiways
Catchin' pieces of the sky between our toes

I miss the way we fuck each other in a cheap motel
I miss your curves, I miss your words
I even miss your smell, and the stories we might tell

Hiway 80 cuts the throats of
Several states before Chicago
Sex and death are best when they get loud
The sun will steal them as its jaws go slack in the
Break of a thunder cloud

Winter comes and I must travel soon
Sterile, stupid, irritated, doomed
I feel like hibernatin', feel my heart is achin', hope you are o.k.
And that you call me sometime soon
I hope you call me soon

FLESH AND BLOOD
Ann Arbor MI 1998

I'm in love with your blood
I'm in love with your bones
I'm in love with your flesh
And what it has become

How I long for your touch
And to feel your embrace
Like a dog I know your scent
Memorized your taste

Every little star that shines
Fills the sky with your light

You set my soul on fire

NO LIGHT
Ann Arbor MI 2002

I saw the saddest thing I've ever seen today
I saw a man whose light had gone away
He wouldn't know the sun if it were to shine
He wouldn't see a ray of light at all
He wouldn't know the rain if it were to fall
He hardens like a stone but you don't mind
You should have made some true friends in this world

Everything you said is forgotten now
The memory doesn't hold much water now
Someone could walk in at any time
And find you in the spotlight all alone
Would you reach if someone threw a line?
Or is your sadness all you call your own?
You should have made some true friends in this world

Papa, where you going?
Don't forget your light.

GOT TO GET OUT
Ypsilanti MI 1999

I been sittin' here by the roadside
Feelin' like my only friend died
I can't find a soul to give me a ride
I'm sick to the death of life

Have another smoke the world ends
Leave behind a string of girlfriends
Go somewhere and let my heart mend
I'm sick to the death of life

Told you that I love you but I lied
Broken from the times I tried
Your quest for my heart has been denied
I'm sick to the death of life

Drink myself into a hole
To fill a void that's in my soul
I try to stay cool but I lose control
I'm sick to the death of life

Feel like my life has been in vain
All the days just end up the same
I ain't got a dollar to my name
I'm sick to the death of life

Run as far as I can get from home
Rot in hell and die and alone
You know the maggots and the worms gonna pick my bones
I'm sick to death of life
I gotta get out
Can't get out

CRYIN' BLUES
Ypsilanti MI 1998

Said to my baby you know that aint right
Come up to love you I just get a fight
There was a time when you was my heart's delight
I fall in darkness and crawl for the light

Said to my baby well I had enough
You leave me hung over feelin' so rough
The way you love me if you love me at all
Cause me to stumble I stumble and fall

I'm bleedin' and I'm dyin' and I'm cryin' inside over you
Why'd you go away and leave me for dead?

SONG FOR THE CROW
Ann Arbor MI 1996

Crow spent a year and a day
Pecking at her shadow
Dark thing has come alive
Swallowed her whole
Now she's dead

Broke the glass, surrendered
But the vase remembers
Fire burns to embers
Then comes alive
Chained to survive

Chained to survive
Do you know what that's like?

LAY IT ON DOWN
Olympia WA 1995

No more water left in the well
All you got's been shot to hell
Make a circle now in the sky
Sun goes down and it's time to fly

You wanna ride, son, you got to pay
Shake my pockets down for loose change
Oh, you know I'm so goddam broke
Goes through my fingers, all up in smoke

Lay it on down, you know it aint no sin
Don't know when I'll be back this way again
On the road, I'm out the door
When it's all you got, it means so much more

Time's a'wastin', no time to kill
Lay it on down, yeah you know I will

DON'T FUCK WITH ME WHEN I'M SHEDDING
Ypsilanti MI 1998

Don't fuck with me when I'm shedding—it's not safe
Don't fuck with me when I'm shedding—it's not safe

When you turn around
I'll bite you in the back of your fucking head
When I'm through with you
You're gonna wish yeah wish yeah wish
You were dead

Don't fuck with me when I'm eating—it's not safe
Don't fuck with me when I'm eating—it's not safe

When you turn around
I'll bite you in the back of your fucking head
When I'm through with you
You're gonna wish yeah wish yeah wish
You were dead

I wanna bigger cage!
I wanna bigger house!
I want my water changed!
I wanna eat a mouse!

CAGE
Ypsilanti MI 1998

I'm looking through your eyes
Like I'm looking through the bars of my cage
I'm looking through your eyes
Like I'm looking through the bars of my cage
You might be just a girl
But you're gonna be a woman some day

I hate the things I have
Just to see them makes me blue
I hate the things I have
Because they all remind me of you
But I love this road I'm on
Because it takes me away from you

Now I found a new thing
And I can't feel pain at all
Now I found a new thing
And I can't feel pain at all
I'm gone, gone, gone
Don't bother to write or call

SO COOL, SO CAL, SO FUCKING WHAT
Phoenix AZ 2010

Get on your roller blades
Get on your Segways
Go to a beach that's covered in trash and bums
Wouldn't that be fun?

They like a speed freak
They like a litter bug
No smoking signs and the clothing must stay on
The cops took away my bong

I want the outside, baby
Can't get away if you don't leave it behind
So Cool SoCal
So Cool So Cal So Fucking What

They like a rush hour
They like a glass tower
They like their Eddie Bauers glistening in the sun
But the city is just no fun

Take me to the earthquake baby
You can take me to the quake
So Cool SoCal
So Cool So Cal So Fucking What

LAST OF THE WILD SONS
Ypsilanti MI 1997

Now I've built this web
Its strands are known to none
Known to none but me
In its knot I am set free

Throw your innocence away
Wasn't that a Golden Age?
Throw your innocence away
Never had it anyway

Last of the wild sons
Cut me loose and let me run
Sing yourself a golden song
Tied me up but not for long